RACHEL MENNIES, SERIES EDITOR

WALT MCDONALD FIRST-BOOK PRIZE · WINNER ·

Also in the series:

OVERBURDEN

POEMS

JOLENE BRINK

TEXAS TECH UNIVERSITY PRESS

This book is typeset inAdobe Caslon Pro. The paper used in this book meets the minimum requirements of ANSI/NISO Z39.48-1992 (R1997). ∞

Designed by Hannah Gaskamp
Cover design by Hannah Gaskamp

Library of Congress Cataloging-in-Publication Data

Names: Brink, Jolene author. Title: Overburden: Poems / Jolene Brink
Description: Lubbock, Texas: Texas Tech University Press, 2026. | Series:
Walt McDonald First-book Prize in Poetry | Summary: "A poetry collection documenting and elegizing the aftermath of extraction and the compulsion to put something back in"—-Provided by publisher.
Identifiers: LCCN 2025044386 (print) | LCCN 2025044387 (ebook) |
ISBN 978-1-68283-302-5 paperback | ISBN 978-1-68283-303-2 ebook
Subjects: LCGFT: Poetry Classification: LCC PS3602.R531825 O94 2026
(print) |
LCC PS3602.R531825 (ebook)
LC record available at https://lccn.loc.gov/2025044386
LC ebook record available at https://lccn.loc.gov/2025044387

Texas Tech University Press
Box 41037
Lubbock, Texas 79409-1037 USA
800.832.4042
ttup@ttu.edu
www.ttupress.org

for Leo & Gus

The overburden is piled in great masses over rich deposits, which the miner cannot work until this mass of debris is moved.

—*REPORT BOOK FOR MINING ENGINEERS*, 1896

Cook it with rainwater in a stone vessel for three hours.
Then purify it carefully, and dissolve it in Aqua Regis,
which is composed of equal parts of vitriol, nitre, and sal ammoniac.
Another formula is vitriol, saltpetre, alum, and common salt.

—PARACELSUS

So, the past is always within us. It's the invisible, mysterious continent that you sometimes feel when you're half-awake. A continent with mountains and seas that constantly influences the weather and the shades of light within you.

—JON KALMAN STEFANSSON

CONTENTS

FOREWORD

"Just try to put it back," exhorts the speaker at the outset of *Overburden*, Jolene Brink's stunning debut collection. Just try—but we never can again. There is no return, throughout this book, to a landscape untouched by a heavy human hand, to a *before*: before a child is born or miscarried; before the earth is destroyed for its minerals and before the subsequent climate destruction; before the born child watches the world on fire from his window.

Note the passive voice that so often accompanies these questions about irrevocable change: who's the destroyer, the creator, the agent of rupture? *Overburden* answers through a vital lyric historicization of mining in Minnesota and its ongoing stakes, both human and natural, within a broader ecopoetic rendering of the American Northwest and Upper Midwest as they burn and melt, respectively, from manmade interventions.

In *Overburden*, Brink also maps the story of the speaker's sons' arrivals and a preceding pregnancy loss. The boys' entrance in the collection shows us the perhaps-futility of attempts to distinguish between "human" and "natural" forces, especially in cases of childbirth, where the mysteries of gestational growth and failure-to-grow reside somewhere in between. "I can't separate our inventions / from the muddy streams around us," notes the speaker of "When Flight 235 Crashes into the Keelung River."

Brink explores this tension directly in the long poem "Report Book for Mining Engineers"—one of my favorite poems in the collection and one of its most dazzlingly ambitious—where multiple definitions of *overburden* collide and interweave:

> In the Mine there are .... tons of ore in sight, having
> an average value of .... to children playing in the fields.
> . . .
> One day, the mine picked up the entire town

and moved it to remove the ore underneath.

Here, we witness the interwoven cycle of violence and growth via the image of the town literally heaved up—overburdened—to take more from the earth; the town where children play hoisted into the sky; the town where the parents of those children live and survive thanks to the existence of the mine, whose resources keep them alive, but which ruins the earth beneath the overburden itself. It is unsustainable in every sense, the "antithesis of nature," says the speaker, and yet the practice has sustained mankind for centuries, become vital in its own way to the survival of our species—due in part to other human evils. As the speaker notes: "There are niches in Greek mines where slaves placed their lanterns."

So what are we to do, lifted above and buried underneath the overburden, implicated as part of the "ouroboros biting its tail," as the speaker writes in "Report . . ."? This question is central to *Overburden* and becomes richest, and most damning, in the collection's poems about motherhood. "Could you bring a child into a world predicted to burn? / Could you offer them a world in new growth and ashes?" the speaker asks in "The Quickening," another incredible long poem. We know from earlier pages that, in the universe of the book, the question is not rhetorical: two children are born, and another lost, within it. As a result, the speaker works to reconcile her fears about the future with her desire for one that includes not only her sons' existence but also their safety.

Brink's speaker is pregnant during the pandemic, and the poems that chart this era of her life are tinged with a piercing loneliness and a new layer of fear—one of contagion. "I always thought I would let you go into the world. But we are losing practice," she writes in "Dear Pandemic Baby." "We never intended this solitude to last." The speaker's "pandemic baby" is her first living child, but in the poem "Do You Have Any Children?", we meet all three, including the one heartbreakingly lost before birth:

I keep one in a birch grove. A bed of moss.
No, you can believe me. I placed her
on that moss next to running water
where I kept the birds singing—begged them,
keep her—as I turned away.

Returned to the earth, the lost daughter blurs the collection's human and natural demarcations; we visit her, "moss-colored," later in the poem, with the speaker's youngest son, a devastating moment that points both forward into a precarious future and backward into a loss-tinged past. And—whether from grief or joy, or both—just as the earth opens, whether for mining or for new growth, the speaker says, "I asked them all to break me open."

As a new parent, I feel this line at my core: there is an inevitability, during pregnancy, of *what comes next*, the knowledge that one can never again *just put it back*; the overburden has not yet been breached, but it is working, growing, hopefully sustaining. In the subsequent and precarious *after*, once the birthing body has broken, but held, the infant sleeping in arms beside a window overlooking another too-warm summer (and, in Chicago in 2025, one also marked with Canadian wildfire smoke, burning for months on end), the weight of *after*'s responsibility could break us.

But *Overburden* resists, deftly, either fatalism or too-easy optimism at the sight of what's underneath the overburden. Instead, Brink offers us resilience, as every living thing on earth must find: for, as the speaker of "Lolo Pass" tells us, "everyone stops here before they keep going."

RACHEL MENNIES

OVERBURDEN

I.

THE PRESENT SEASON

The microscope necessary for seeing is in the other room.

Both points contain the same amount of light.

These judgements are easily broken in half.

The specimen is doubtful but joyous.

But the abundance is ready to proceed.

It is quite possible to go on collecting forever.

The present season is rolling in with fog.

JUST TRY TO PUT IT BACK

As for returning the land to a shape without settlement, start with the lower meadow white with frost, and loganberries low on the branch. Start with green grass hip-high with nettle, narrow leaves split below apple blossom, dead creek tree wrapped in moss, the cut grass coming back. Start where someone left off—buildings torn down, edges overgrown, this one edible, this one repaired, this trail follows the property line, this leads under the trees named for your children. They are returning from the city. They are trying to remember you as anything but this. They cannot.

HARUSPEX

This ancient practice of gathering figs.

A warm bowl of milk. Things you cannot swallow.

Leaving your house. Fields flooded with storm.

The lakes rising in our sleep.

These nights I dream about a road you creep along
but cannot love.

Lost in mid-sentence I asked for you and came up with bones.

Nobody is okay with what is missing.

Our job is to find a narrative that heals.

These words will not leave your room.

This wax is holding you together.

Please take these words from me and rise another way.

SHOUT POUCH CABIN, EUGENE, OREGON

I fear all of this is going faster than we'd planned.

The horses grazing below the interstate.
The trees planted beside the clear cut.

Your journal says: *lupine in the meadow six feet tall.*
We find: rusted cans & cow bones,

a pair of old bachelors with crooked teeth,
another couple who didn't last the winter.

When you said, *what if we put it all back now?*
Was it the heavy plantings of cedar and fir,

or copper wire absorbed by alder branch?
Was it these bright things, these veined hands?

What if we clarify the request?

That the return equals the taking
and the clear cut become a ritual.

To get here you need
an interstate and a nostalgia.

The ghosts are waiting in the driveway.
I will carry all the things you've lost.

Buttons and photographs, eyesight and young knees.

Franz, I heard you on the stairs last night,
waiting out the storm. *Keep going back*, you said.

I am so tired of disappearing places.

THEN THE WIND

A man has one body,
so solitary

inside the curtains.

The soul is sick of this solid sheath.

And a room that doesn't need you. But you keep it

with ears and eyes the size of buttons
and skin, a mass of
scars, a skeleton's robe.

Put it on, then. From somewhere else
fly through the cornea   *to the icy spoke,*
                               to the bird's chariot
                               to the heavenly spring.

You know this
through its prison bars.
    Before remembering
        it hears
        without asking,
            the clamor of woods,
            some lilac on the table.

        What you tasted last. What you replied to.
        If you only knew
        how *I dream of*
        it and cannot stop.

WHEN FLIGHT 235 CRASHES INTO THE KEELUNG RIVER

So that we who stand on shore
without arms long enough to reach the survivors

say I can see them waving back.
I recognize their lives packed in floating suitcases.

All morning I watch the rubber rafts stir up the river.
I can follow the emergency workers circling the fuselage

or pour my cold coffee down the drain
as the video streams footage.

Searchlights passing over military uniforms
study the dead machine like a metal coin

shoved down the throat of a city seized with
industry and warning lights.

Each of the things
we created catching up with us.

I can't separate our inventions
from the muddy streams around us.

I want to mourn both worlds we split open
on the shoreline looking over the wreckage.

I disturbed these waters by watching.
Or, what I lost when I turned away.

11

The river before the rescue,
the city before the crushed metal,
the flight patterns below the current.

ST. JOHN'S UNIVERSITY

This is what I found underneath:
the bleached bones of a bear, the outline
of a cabin caved into limestone, a dozen lives wandering
down the animal path. What are we looking for
    when we turn them over?
In one story the German monks arrived at dawn
carrying manuscripts and cast-iron pots. In one story
they tamed the bear and penned him up, outside the monastery,
or buried his bones at the edge of the prairie.

    If I take their buildings apart, stone by stone
back to the quarry, the papers fling themselves into the sky
and the monks stumble backwards searching for the road.

Nobody told me dreaming back the highway was a trespass,
    but I rolled it up each night.
It went like the road makers into the last century,
backwards down the slick tar cutting open the grass.
    I took away the train tracks too, with passengers
    waving like thin reeds in crimped moss hats.
    The past a restless light
crossing the prairie.

WASPS IN THE APPLE TREE

They hang slick with penance
riding our fruit into the ground.

Earthbound it's all we can do.
They whirl toward us.

Apple planets fill the grass
with zest made of wings.

This fruit is borrowed (see: lent)
grammatically correct (see: rented)

The pact is removal, then denial.
You keep collecting this year,

but last year too, and a decade later
holes shrunk down

where they tunneled at night
wings curled back to fit against the seeds.

GRAFT

Today, the present work—

Furnish the roots with vigor.
This graft is trying to see what holds.

Where does the stock take its first cut?
You need at least one good eye to follow.

That is,
the weight
has no consequence
if we know where to begin.

That is, the affinity between species,
the quince and the horse chestnut,
wild cherry and currant,
are also tenderness of time.

Soil in repose. Multiplicity of belonging.

Let loose an enumeration of trees.

Sap in the open air.

It cannot be the same this time around.

FIRST WOMAN TO CIRCLE GLOBE SOLO, DIES

Somewhere not far away a war was being fought . . .
but from the sky above, all looked peaceful.

—JERRIE MOCK

You stepped onto land   *the sky over Vietnam*
where the crowd was waiting   *casual blue without war*
& asked you how you felt   *the first woman*
& who cleaned the house   *the first woman*
& your future ex-husband   *so far alone*
leaned in for the kiss   *miles & miles & miles*

PAST LIFE #1

The woman   with cat eyes stares out of photographs
    from hallways   in the dusk   she bends in her chair. She
cannot break the rules anymore.

Our eyes crossed   listening for a heartbeat.   In another life,
I built her a silent retreat in the forest.

In this life I know   when I haven't been here.   She tells me
    her first   life is stuck
behind a pane of glass,   the other lives pressed against it.
    Both sides weigh   the same. She tells me

her baptism skin is   red dress camouflage the skin she untied
    beneath pine trees waving back   the skin that tried to
    run floating out of reach.   They promise she'll   be
happy with this   rebirth   each time she remembers.

PAST LIFE #2

old cracked things without flicker   impulse

things that have been for a long time

a long path   people walking away from the shipwreck

   salt to whomever turns

water underneath what is lost…old things: coins hard as char
  the brittle hand who exchanged it first   who turned

around under the ship: more sea   how many lives since

the first wave dusted us   no ark no lingering

this time   bodies   next to go   words

II.

PRIMA MATERIA

I felt the world from every angle, especially below the surface.

I fell through to pull the light back out
and found worms wrapped around the planet.

I could hear the Renaissance dragging her fingers
through the dirt a millennia before she arrived.

I saw the moon boarded by women without wings
and Mandragora root disguised as turmeric in the grocery store.

I put everything I couldn't taste into a jar
and buried it at the crosswalk.

It's the smell of the dead ones on the stairs before calling them back.

Or, what you can't see behind wet clouds in front of the sun.

Or, if you keep pulling out your hair,
it's the thing you hope to find underneath.

SOPHIE BRAHE, 1594

Her position as an occasional assistant to Tycho Brahe
makes her of some importance to the history of science.
—MARILYN BAILEY OGILVIE

Dear Brother,

When I heard you say *bury the sun*,
I let the stars pass through my hands.

Little alembic seeds.
Vowels soaked in brine.

You said—
      they will not find us here,
then promised copper & seed pass through the ground
when we wait long enough,

Brother, you said
      opacity takes 800,000 light-years to reach us.

Clearly, this is no place for a prolonged stay.
The whole structure hostage to our gaze.
You built the telescope, but I put our stars on the page.

I keep watching the clouds spit green into the sea.
I tried pulling something tangible out of the sky.
I tried preoccupation but it dissolved.
I laughed when I saw the planets move.
I used their coordinates to entertain our guests.
I traced the shipwrecks wrapped in fog.

Nobody suspects your boredom here,
or my lust for this routine:
brushing sand off the lens,
    chipping back the universe,
fine-tuning the elements.

O tender lights,
I've been waiting for so long to see—

When I learned a telescope was an instrument for collecting
our own thoughts what did you expect?

INTERVIEW WITH A MINING ENGINEER JUST NOW REALIZING THE PROPERTY UNDER DISCUSSION APPEARS TO BE A GLACIER

Tell them the frost flowers
are blooming with brine
    and the bedrock does not conform.

Tell them there are meteorites still burning on the surface.

The exact location of the mine
can be found on any good map.

This is what glaciers do—
    release the horses
        clean the kitchen floor
make ice cubes for the dinner party.

In 1777, a silver Roman ingot weighing 11 oz.
was discovered when new foundations
were poured for the Tower of London.

How did it get there,
    Or, what did it accumulate by trying?

It should be ascertained
whether there is any dispute for the
possession of the property.

So much for the change of the seasons.
There is………. indebtedness or encumbrance
against the property if we put everything we own
in alphabetical order.

See: Debris, *accumulation*
        Rigid-body, *rotation*
        Surface, *debris*
        Toe, *of glacier*

It is extremely difficult
to imagine how we could possibly take
anything more from the surface.

INTERVIEW WITH A PLANET NOBODY REALIZED WAS HIDING BEHIND THE SUN

How long were you planning to keep this up?

> Given the choice, I might leave,
> but I like it here.

Tell us about the sun.

> Burn up once
> and then return
>   do it all over again.

How did you avoid getting noticed for so long?

> The radio says the age of discovery is not yet over,
> so keep trying.

You were listening to our radios?

> And bent stalks of corn, and satellites
> and the next generation preparing
> to enter the atmosphere.

What can you see from over there?

> Everything
> dropping into open
> mouths.

INTERVIEW BETWEEN A PLANET AND THEIR DOCTOR

Exercising regularly?

I never get the same weight twice.

Looks like it's been a while since we checked your eyes.

I keep blinking and blinking and blinking.

What's this?

A piece of tin in my atmosphere.

And your love life?

Like trying to escape the moon.

INTERVIEW WITH A MAN WHO KNOWS THE MONA LISA IS FOLLOWING HIM

They say our earliest cells dredged the sea for light.

See how we're still devouring the sun?

Towards the end of his life
Da Vinci carried the Mona Lisa everywhere.

Today, a national committee reported finding symbols
in the darkest part of her iris.

Do you believe them?

Her eyes let me know something is still watching.
I don't need your experts to see embedded narratives.

Listen, when Jeanne Calment turned 122, she recalled
selling paint to Vincent van Gogh in 1888.

She said he was dirty, badly dressed and disagreeable.

But look what collected there along the fringe of a single memory.

I want to pull out the symbols da Vinci placed in those eyes.

Now a new committee calls those symbols cracks,
caused by aging and shapes subject to overinterpretation.

Just watch the way she moves.

PROFILE OF ANTIMONY

Antimony is a small town that grows corn.
Every year another city block disappears.

Today the shuttered market
apologizes for its lack of tides

and cultural capital, here in this place
named for an atomic state that means *not alone*.

Alchemists like to say transmutation
when they really mean *collision of things seen*.

In a drawing from 1617 antimony is a wolf
attacking a soldier. The river travels past both.

We are meant to see passion
paired with anxiety.

We are meant to see, even then,
an element painfully aware of her needs.

PROFILE OF A GLACIER

When she is late for class the tardy bell widens her fissures.

They stare at her from across the lunchroom.
Nobody will trade sandwiches.

Strangers like to touch her when she is distracted by the
sunrise. They ask her if she has any other shades of blue
besides the one she is currently wearing.

The frozen hunter holding a spear prods her spine whenever
she does a downward dog. She knew his name once but not
where he came from. Sometimes they trade jokes.

When the poles shift she asks *did anyone else feel that*?
But they just keep walking.

She goes to the gym and reads *Cosmopolitan* because the
doctor says she needs more muscle. Afterwards she drags her
feet home and closes all the shades.

PROFILE OF AN ALCHEMIST

In track practice the coach mouthed *let go* when she trailed
behind the other runners.

She believed the analogy of a brick wall holding back her
thighs was accurate enough.

If she leapt over permission her muscles would understand
the next dimension was elemental.

*

Because she married young her heart is deciphered whenever
she says *husband* and elusive when she uses *partner*.

Her heart is soliciting spare rooms
for a future where nobody is lonely.

It feels sleepy when strangers say *spouse* at a party with
chocolate éclairs nobody is brave enough to eat.

*

Her heart multiplies the years they've been together
by the number of rooms in the house.

One sounds like a closet. One closes the kitchen door.
Alternatively there is a soup pot

too big to cook anything
except on Sundays.

REPORT BOOK FOR MINING ENGINEERS, 1895

The writer of the foregoing report is expected to fill in the blank pages at the end of the book with his own words and ideas.

—ARTHUR GEORGE CHARLETON

1.

Fill in the blank.

The elevation of the Mine is .... feet higher than .... and .... feet above sea level. There are ....…..…... species of birds circling the mountain.

2.

Is the property under dispute?

When Cortez arrived Moctezuma gave him gold, women, and clothing.

When the Siphnians forgot to feed their gods, Apollo flooded the mines.

Homer had no word for metal.

3.

Is the outcrop of the vein exposed at the surface?

Is the vein an artery, a circumnavigation, a deposit-soaked brine?

Is the outcrop visible from .... miles away?

Blood vessels running underground,
a constant set of points with length but no thickness.

We are amazed at the origin of our own definitions.

4.

Are white ants or other insect pests common?

See: gold, silver, platinum tucked underground
        timber comes from rooms comes from ants
        colonies of white ants mulching cellulose

Check your wooden beams. The damage caused by termites
        costs Southwestern states $1.5 billion every year.

In Australia scientists are studying termites to discover gold
        deposits.

See: Proverbs 6:6

5.

Fill in the blank.

In the Mine there are .... tons of ore in sight, having
an average value of .... to children playing in the fields.

6.

What is the duty of a miner's inch in this ground?
    Ask yourself—

Which fracture of rock would you choose?

What accumulation of history shines more?

The gold on the bottom of Moctezuma's feet,

Or Nike Women's Classic Cortez Leather shoes for $70.00?

7.

At any rate, the writer desires to point out that some of the conclusions present here
were reached a long time ago.

There are niches in Greek mines where slaves placed their lanterns.

We built our desire on tin, nimbus, golden gravel.

Little cartridge of centuries.

There isn't just one tide coming to turn over your history.

8.

See that there are ample reserves in sight.

They beat the ore small.

Select experienced men.

Antithesis of nature.

Individualism and energy are flywheels of progress.

The use of native copper
marks the beginning
of every ancient metal culture.

9.

At any rate can this reduction be effected in a single operation or gradually?

The ores of this property are suitable for reduction
by .... starting with the King of Spades.

This is an unauthorized facsimile of the earth.

The uses for copper and silver are endless.

The list of missing people throughout history is endless:

Oct 22, 1989
Jacob Erwin Wetterling disappears in Cold Spring, Minnesota
There are cameras with black cords in the mud.
His mother wears a yellow dress with shoulder pads.

1483 AD
The two Princes in the Tower.

71 BC
If Spartacus fakes his death
there is nothing to bury him with.

1581 AD
A deck of French playing cards reveal
Henry III holding a fan. The Queen
the scepter. The Princes are nowhere.

Oct 22, 1989
Dogs still searching the cornfields.

10.

*What stock of tools will be required for carrying out operations
on the scale being proposed?*

Begin by reinstating the purged monsters.
The basilisk and the plastic saints.
The men at the bottom of a Norwegian fjord.
The griffin claws sold on the black market disguised
    as mammoth tusks.

Begin where Pliny left off.

Disbelieving the Sirens only inspires virgins
to wilt faster (but the unicorns
can tell the difference, as any fair
and proper monster could).

When Cortez fell off his horse,
Moctezuma's men saw monsters too.

Something subdivided the glaciers.
Something pre-industrial went to sleep.
Something drained the glacial lake without asking.

11.

To this, however, must be added any cash or other realizable assets
    there may be,
and the "present value" of the price that may be fetched at the end of
    the mine's life.

I realize until recently the world's largest lake was under a
    sheet of ice.

Ask yourself,
    what do the Nile and Mississippi sound like
    if you put them together?

    If you flood a valley where no one is looking?

See: Metallurgy (*not* Melancholy)
    Tin (*not* Timing)
    Assay (*not* Assemblage)

12.

Fill in the blank.

The parties will sell .... payable in ....
installments to the nearest .... devouring itself.

See: The ouroboros biting its tail.

13.

Fact: the PolyMet sulfide mine
is lauded for the economic benefits
it will provide northern Minnesota
for the next twenty years.

(shallow steps, plunge faster)

Quality: the Ojibwe harvesting wild rice from Birch Lake

Quality: who have been here all along

Your question might be?

14.

Where has the world's supply been chiefly obtained, and disposed;
and what is the present estimated world's stock of metal on hand?

Ingenious laboratory, this nature.

The rice grows on its own.

In 2050 BC the only iron available
in Babylonia came from stray meteors.
(Early star gazers, beware)

In 1948, serious interest
developed around the spot
where you're now sitting,
but explorations failed to find
any significant deposits worth revisiting—

In 2009, the proposed PolyMet mine
was opened for public review.

Fact: they built it for jobs
Quality: centuries of nearby waters

Fact: In 1475 BC Thutmose III goes to war
riding a chariot made from
33% silver and 67% gold

(we see his wife
trailing behind, green carbonate of copper
around her wrists)

15.

*The things that grow in the earth all assimilate themselves to the
earth.*

Sometimes the men my grandfather hired
at his gravel pit found gold pebbles in the gravel.

Hippocrates told physicians they should examine
where the winds came from
whenever they arrived in an unfamiliar town.

Once my grandfather's men found a mammoth tusk in the
gravel.
The photograph shows them standing with their discovery.
The local museum added it to their glass case of prehistoric
artifacts.

See: They put it back.

16.

The gravel pit office was a square, single-story building on the edge of town. Inside the office my aunts batched orders and rang up sales. Outside pile of dirt and rock towered over everything. Sometimes the men unloaded their extra cement into the swamp nearby. It was faster than bringing it elsewhere.

They were thinking about children, dinner, paychecks.

See: They put it back.

See: Drain pipe, water filter, ecosystem, inheritance.

17.

Is labor abundant, locally, or otherwise, and of what class?

I grew up two hours from the Hull Rust Mine in Hibbing, Minnesota.

Bob Dylan is also from Hibbing.

2 miles wide
535 feet deep
700 million tons of ore hauled away since 1895

Their high school auditorium had gilded ceilings.
The mine wanted educated workers.

One day, the mine picked up the entire town
and moved it to remove the ore underneath.

THE STARS IN THEIR COURSES

whatever this life is, it shews a strange capacity for reproducing itself
—SIR JAMES JEANS

Given the choice I would go further: rub the metal
ridges of Pluto: put my heels on another atmosphere

and rebound towards the stars. In a single generation
the earth slipped into our palms. A millennium of field

work carving open prairies, turning guns out of fires.
The radio says the age of discovery is not over, we

are plummeting to the cellular level, mixing our soup
of electrons and electricity with our satellite passing Pluto,

the last threshold in our lifetime, sending back photos like
the first daguerreotype processed in backrooms

and later on, the desert floor, the mountain cliff,
ink scratching out the landscape: imagine carrying

away the likeness of a place that never looks
the same way twice.

% GDP, OF

1. Whatever Greeks believed were inside those clouds.

2. Literacy rates for a sinking island in the Pacific.

3. Milking machines sitting unused in Argentina.

4. Cows standing in the field.

5. The same year a sinking island imported a dozen encyclopedias without a single misspelled word.

6. Undercounted illiterate dreams.

7. Red cars moving in the same direction.

8. Perseus counting passing trees, but nothing else.

FROM THE BEGINNING

See: division of time (beginning as era)
          a place or abode (beginning as home)
          a very long time (beginning as once)

          Some will not know age. It outlasts them.

          We learned to see age when it was already upon us.
          In Eden age was the uppermost branch.
          The inevitable (not death) the dying (but)—

          In Eden it snowed when we looked the other way,
               cold afterthought, right behind us.

See: it comes suddenly to the ground

          snowfall, downfall, fallacy

          And you look up—
          Standing face to face with the missing.

          This is not a question standing on its own.

See: making, losing, showing (all the same)
          the rock you're clinging to (all the same)
          time dictates all else (same the same)

          In Eden every face was a face was faceless.

We learned age by counting missing branches,
missing lights, missing snow, until missing time appeared.

Or, what appeared was subject to time
    was turning our backs to the snow, not dying, but—

ALCHEMY

She was split open by ether and dew.

Around here we wear turtlenecks without makeup. The basis
of beauty is the undertow that took your sister.

Skin is thinnest under your eyelids, thickest at the
bottom of your feet. Some days she walks barefoot across the
Hardee's parking lot with french fries in a paper bag: grease
with salt and seagull. In another life: *antimony, quicksilver,
gold*. In another life she would sleep with four abbots,
rotating their chipped fingernails fidgeting with her hair. We
want her to steal everything from them. Instead, they dipped
her in *Mercury of Saturne*. She is suspected of burning the
fields, of casting *Salt of Kali* into the eyes of passing soldiers.
What they did to keep her together, when underneath she
was already red tincture (meaning: *like dissolves like*).

//

She is so tired of being pulled out of the ground.
Medical texts praise her luster,
her application will drive your lips rouge,
will turn your tin plate additives into chemical
page turners. Alloy emerging via the global scene,
tipped into buckets, feel the ocean lift
under this molten core.

She is an occurrence, memorized into pigments stacking
oxygen onto the cheeks of women
crossing the street with their leather purses.

See how they pulse? See her application
among the other elements hanging nearby,
the street corners watching. She is aware
of her instability. Who will make her a catalyst?

Ions bloom like pigeons pulling
up from park benches. Under a microscope
everything is tangible if you sing.

The drug of choice is enamel and she claws it
to pieces, slightly less than arsenic
she weighs herself each morning, measuring
her toxicity against the numbers
assigned to her body.

You can look in the text
book to learn when she was first
    isolated, just like that, first believed whole.

                    //

C. G. Jung saw squares repeating themselves. He hid copper
pieces behind the ceiling tiles of his office, heard them pulse
whenever patients described cannons going off inside their salt
    shakers. (Other things traded on the Silk Road: *jade, tea
philosophy, disease*).

The modern mind is readable if you place a mirror
    at the back of its tongue. The basis of hypnosis requires
a pure heart and serving of dragon blood. You get to pick
which extinction you prefer,
    whether Thales of Miletus
really predicted the solar eclipse during a naval battle
(they were already fighting in the dark)

or the Chinese discovered gunpowder
searching for the elixir of life.

Jung kept samples of lead beneath his tongue, sweetened with
wine. He told his patients *put these rocks in your pocket*,
here is a gold coin with etchings rubbed off. Underneath
is the recipe for *Prima Materia.*

You too can make your own Philosopher's Stone using everyday
household items.

Just keep licking your lips whenever I clap my hands.

Now tell me what you see.

III.

REVOLUTIONS OF THE HEAVENLY SPHERES

Dear symmetry and vanity,
I am like so many growing planets.

I am shaped by expectation and choice.
This is not gravity.

The other women see all of me.
Are we meant to glow like beautiful orbs?

This recivilization. This child
inside of me awake and hungry.

I want fresh orange juice
and a week floating in the ocean,

I walk airport terminals
watching the ones who survived.

So what if we came
from the stars?

The planets still pull themselves apart
looking for a way out.

FOR GUTHRIE

All these things tethered to me. Unpaid bills and unanswered texts. The tomatoes green under the fog. This summer you and I are never apart. This summer I look for you in every passing bird. Let it be a sign you'll stay and then, let it be a sign you'll arrive. This motherhood is not a tomb to any former self. I am remaking her each morning. Where is the welcoming song nobody taught me to sing?

MOTHERLODE #1

The alchemist knows everything she produces will fill rooms she
   cannot afford.

Rent went up at the beginning of the month. Who will store
   these secrets?

Who will inherit these buckets of copper filings, antimony mixed
   in mason jars?

The lawyers are telling her to name everything, but the elements
   keep changing.

Some count themselves twice. Others appear at the window
   admiring the mountains.

FIRE SEASON

The bullet arriving from a previous century
    doesn't know which way to go.
Smoke lapped the continent while we slept.
We flew across the ocean.
We shrugged our shoulders into the satellites.

*

We gave birth to false stars and took misdirection for truth.
Plume of language. Once, we spoke in ashes while the sun wavered.
This is not the form of destruction we would choose for ourselves.
Just say it won't happen and keep your head down.

*

Woman with water vessel and aching bones.
Woman with child folding herself into a mountain.
Imagine the fire will go there where we can't follow.
Don't swallow those songs of praise just yet.

THIRD TRIMESTER

Fog in the garden.

The heat elsewhere.

Wild lupines tip forward.

Tourists flock the shoreline.

Everywhere signs of arrival.

Everywhere pigeon wings.

The barometer drops.

The tenth marigold blooms.

What more can I offer?

The neighbor mowing her lawn.

Curtains hush the kitchen.

The dishes drying.

Nobody knows your name.

PAST LIFE #3

everything has to go somewhere   the pages of the novel
   century-old cement block
left against the neighbor's fence   it has to go
somewhere or it stays
except the moss on a red oak   trying to catch the smell
   of the body
going fast   with the soul trailing behind

MAIDENHOOD & MOTHERHOOD, OR TEN PHASES OF WOMAN'S LIFE, 1886

Became calendar months. Decayed bulletin boards.
Papers sagging. The open razor window. Worn down
even in soft light. It passed for spring.

---

*The case is reported by the learned Dr. Desormeaux, of Paris,
and occurred under his own notice in the Hospital de Maternité
of that city. A woman, the mother of three children, became
insane. Her physician thought that a new pregnancy might
reestablish her intellectual faculties.*

It was wet air passing into the room. It became ritual.
The air entering the room. The mind caught. Say there
was a settled area. A mind they could not trace.

---

*Her husband consented to enter on the register of the hospital
each visit he was allowed to make her, which took place only
every three months. So soon as evidence of pregnancy showed
itself, the visits were discontinued. The woman was confined two
hundred and ninety days after conception.*

The serialized hallways echoing with practical shoes.
The wind flipped pages of a book beside her bed.
What she expected her life would contain. The insanity
of authority and the ritual of waiting.

THE QUICKENING

1.

I wanted to raise a generation without wildfires.
So I put it all off—
motherhood, commitment, whatever a child would replace.

There were good years and bad years when smoke filled our
valley. One season: it leapt from a mountain and crossed
the river. Another: it smoldered in the gulch behind our
house. The smoke jumpers called it an ideal burn—eating
up underbrush but not the upper branches. We watched the
smoke spindle above the larches.

Then the snow fell and we moved on.

Could you bring a child into a world predicted to burn?
Could you offer them a world in new growth and ashes?
It became our game. Peer into the future without blinking.

2.

I volunteered to be stirred in the open air.
I was reduced to surface tension.
I chose to expand my body.

I volunteered myself for little scraps of time.
In my confinement I asked for symmetry and health.
I asked for you to arrive safely.

We were handed a heartbeat that didn't exist.
We put it in a box under the birch trees.

58

I was handed a uterus shaped like a heart.
The doctor untied it and gave it back to me.

3.

I walked into the season of motherhood
when the Flathead cherries bloomed
and the smoke season receded.
When you give birth during a pandemic
it's still you and your body.

When you give birth too early your baby lives
in a square plastic womb outside your body.
And you search the hospital each night for your child
down the hallway, past the masked nurses, inside the pandemic.

4.

I was soaked in old-fashioned ether when you arrived.

It held me down while you convened
with the cult of mothers who didn't make it.

You told them we found the only path out,
waving their ancient dreaming out of the room.

They pulled you from my body
like folded papers from an archive.

THE FIRST LETTING GO

Tell thee, Macduff
was from his mother's
womb untimely ripped.

—*MACBETH*, ACT 5, SCENE 8

Dear Mother,

Let's begin with form,
a cord, a comma—

I know as far ahead as you.
I sense the ghost hands reaching for us.

When we traveled together
my dreams were your outline.

There are ghosts
reaching into us.

Someone's grandmother
Someone's unkept soul
Someone's prediction unleashed

This one will travel in unwrapped circles
This one the size of giants
This one tender as butterfly weed

I knew time like sun passing between clouds

A small forgetting
each time the cloud reappeared

The oldest truth we share
a single longing: to be held
as long as possible.

DEAR PANDEMIC BABY

A vaccine is coming. Winter is barely here, lopsided on the wrong end of the calendar. All those weeks we waited for snow. For you. It comes all at once. Meanwhile, you lean in with thumb and pointer finger for the first time. You are learning to choose without me. You are making your own lessons. There is a buzzing around the space I've held since you were born: little heart, kept tucked away from the world for safekeeping. My breath held all these hours. I always thought I would let you go into the world. But we are losing practice. I didn't mean to keep you hidden for so long. A coaxing spring wavers through the kitchen window. I didn't know what was coming when I invited you inside. We never intended this solitude to last.

LABYRINTH

There was a woman who unfolded her body.

What fell out: *baby teeth*, *dust*, *light*,
Like an army needing order.

Say she asked them to follow,
changed her mind, built a labyrinth.

Say the hedges asked for a name
and she gave them something else.

It looked like a furrowed sky,
wide as Montana that first summer

she was pregnant. How it reached
past her and carried everything away.

Let's say she wanted to be touched that way—again
not by the children in both arms. Not by the lapsed time

between wanting and having. Just the sky and all the things
she could no longer reach.

VERMEER'S MILKMAID, 1657

I too have carried milk at dawn down to the kitchen cradled in bottles over and over again, the endless pouring of oneself into the less terrible day. I too have false solitudes. A learned watching of myself. I've practiced my apologies over this pour. A woman practiced in looking not looking when the young men with their painted smiles and expensive cows pass by my window. Paint me in the most expansive blue. Give me a lead shawl, if you must, keep me alone among my breadcrumbs. Offer up my symbolic ankles and thin fingers and then let me go. I am a mother pouring herself out under the false canvas of your smile. The repetition of my body keeps this child alive.

FOR LEO

Today we took you into the winter afternoon. Sweet
boy high on your father's shoulders.

The wide lake lapped everything into ice. Along the
shoreline cracked by glaciers E. tells us she's pregnant.

A thing so new we rush to measure it. A pea rolling in
her palms. A vowel pushed off the tongue.

I've already forgotten what it took to carry you
anywhere but here, out in the world where later,

you'll cry as your small hands begin to warm, and I
hold them in mine, apologizing.

You were the size of an apple once, I say,
bright, bright inside my body

and we woke together each night
hungry and searching.

MOTHERLODE #2

I want evidence to slide out of me, string of pearls.

Stack me like a set of warm towels.

I want my spheres to align when no one is looking.

She gave birth alone in the river.

She gave birth under a knife.

She gave birth that winter the snows never arrived

and birds circled the house looking for north.

In her intense desire for den light

there was nothing left to confine.

SLEEP TRAINING

I am trying to tell you something. About dawns yoked into nights. About carrying you from your room after midnight. After you wake bumping your head against the soft crib wood. I was dreaming about riding a city bus with strangers to escape the cold. I was rising to put your head in my hands. To protect you from what you cannot see. To hold what you'll need. I forgive you for needing me like this. For breaking the rules they set out for us to follow. One expert says co-sleeping precedes a lifetime of insomnia. Another says, animals, let us slumber together in the warmth of winter. I push back the quilt and hand you into the open tundra of my sheets.

FAIRYTALE #1

Let me leave a trail for you. Hansel and Gretel
went into the forest. The dried breadcrumbs.
The four crows looking the other way. How
they knew their mother's voice. Flowers dull
from watching. Pine needles crowding the path.
I didn't know until I had you what it meant
to send a child alone into the woods.
Only yesterday your new teacher took you
down the hallway into a classroom for toddlers.
She put cheese and crackers on a plate
watching to see who you trusted.

PORTAGE

for Andrea and Brian

We are made to love the sound of flames cracking birch bark open,
to seek crevices of dark water running with snowmelt,
to love what waits for us at dawn. It does not matter
how we arrived. Whether we've portaged
a solo trip upriver, or returned seeking shelter
after a long time living alone. We are made to cross
the lakes together, to go back and revisit old waters.
To sit on the shoreline and wait for the moon to find us.
There are so many words for love: *tinder, cup, bramble*.
So many ways to ask, *are you whole?* And *will you teach me?*
After a long time together, we learn to budget for winters
with bog berries and light scraped from the bottom of a canoe.
We learn to drift inside maps with fading lines, reciting the prayers
of our families and seeking direction from strangers.
We do not forget the quiet spaces stored with awe,
or the signal of a campfire in the distance.

THE SHIPWRECK

We live here on the shore of a lake
so wide it swallows ships and spits back ocean,

the salt water so many miles away
it arrives on the glacial tide as we wade

among the agates and lift you closer
to sun. Your limbs are a tide too,

pulling me in every direction.
Here we walk so we cannot drown.

The oldest shipwreck is there too,
just off the shore where the captain

went down ringing the bell. Sometimes
we hear it in the morning under the sound

of gulls and trains. When you ask,
I tell you *yes, I can hear it too*.

FAIRYTALE #2

Bits of toast, cheap plastic toys. Days
all mine & yours & ours.

How brief green is summer
spaced out between our toes.

Together, we water everything in sight.
Let the climate turn on us,

we are building a fortress of forsythia
and sandcastles.

I don't understand how we hold
so many things without breaking.

But we do. Early smoke season
blinks out the sun. Robins in a nest.

I watch you share berries with a neighbor girl
whose mother reappears to watch you too.

You are casting spells on yourself
while we put food on the table.

You are learning the world is filled
with beavers & unicorns & robins

returning to their homes. I intend
to keep it that way.

FIRST SPRING

It's time to come home now. Time to find our bodies stitched back up. The children are sleeping in their cribs, and we are sitting on the porch. This dry run towards spring. It's time to step outside and let the babies sleep. One of us is widening with sadness. One is homesick for her other body. To know what we've entered into like a trance out here: crows with tilted heads blinking at the sun. To know someday we'll forget this sadness. Replace it with another variant of grief. It has always been that way: this relearning, this circling together after each birth. Someday the children will walk on their own. And keep walking. But that is not our grief, today, flat as the dirt road snow packed by months of travel. We turn our bright necks to see what's coming.

DO YOU HAVE ANY CHILDREN?

I keep one in a birch grove. A bed of moss.
No, you can believe me. I placed her
on that moss next to running water
where I kept the birds singing—begged them,
keep her—as I turned away.

I keep another in an incubator.
That was the place with the chasing clouds.
I kept trying to push him back inside my safety
but he crawled out wanting more. Today he told me
honey comes from bees and nectar comes from flowers
and we sat together eating toast with butter.

I keep the last one on my hip, in the garden,
my shoulders crossing the field. I asked *who are you*
as he arrived and his moss-colored sister
was there. His dead grandmothers were there. Moldering
in their wisdom. His living brother was there.
I asked them all to break me open.
They said, *there is no going back.*

INVENTORY

I used to believe I was keeping it all for myself. This archive filled with the plastic toy dogs you coveted until their painted eyes rubbed off. This cold spring where you watered the snap peas, and rode your bike too far down the alley. Each night you ask about the man who keeps riding his motorcycle down the street before bedtime. The engine an oily blanket over the singing frogs. I confess. I'd keep you tidy as a list on my hip forever if I could. This inventory of nowness. I catch your questions in a mason jar. *Where going? Why loud? How soon?* And now I think it must all be to prove that we were here: the man & the frogs & the wind dark lake.

MOTHERLODE #3

Something else lives inside me now. It asks
for silence in the morning. It has a different hunger.

Try lemon water. Try staples. Try—

I think the frost is pulling back for the last time this season.

I truly believe winter is finally over.
    Heave your shoulders toward me.

A plastic bag roils in the grass.

This is how I name things now:

    watch the world without solace,

    find the things returning,

    pretend sorrow isn't buried
    beside the coneflowers who refuse
    to engage with all this catastrophe.

It's the old philosopher's stone waiting to see
who blinks first. Try me.

IV.

PAST LIFE #4

coins hard as char   the brittle hand who held them
    sand in hollow locks
cracked bones without flicker   a long time below
    no ark, no lingering this time

I play a game called disassembly   it goes
backwards from the beginning
the highway turns to mud   metal & plastic dissolve
    it's easy

nothing goes back the same way   nobody sees the city
disappear
the fog stayed for a week and lifted the snow
    everyone awake in pockets

the river was escaping   the edges refused to give   so the
dark trailed underneath
until it burst   someone running through the fog someone
coming quickly on a bicycle

I TELL YOU, I WANTED TO GET IT RIGHT

But you left your gloves in the kitchen.
You left town with the windows down.
The neighbor saw you in Portland,
but you weren't listening.
Let me put something in the air.
I can't remember why I wanted to be seen.
Or, how you wanted to be safe.
What a few words provided.

&

I tell you I wanted to get it right.
I put all of my faith into aspens.
I turned yellow wishing.
Then, in the dream you tell me
about all the men you loved.
We had coffee by the river.
I am so sick of hiding from that story.

&

I tell you the order matters.
First you see your mother in the mirror.
Then you wish her back.
She paid a man to knead her grief into a village,
then he set her upright again.
I wanted a window with a responsible view.
I watched the sunset harden again our skin.
I meant for you to last.

FOR MY STUDENT WHO LOVES CEPHALOPODS

The world as you know it
has always been kiltered, wompish, like a signaled frenzy
searching for homeplace.

Wild things then, must be lurking
in the dreams
mucked up by all of our tinkering.

A poetry teacher told me once
to write past what I believed was the stopping
point here. To find the poem beyond what I could see.

In a bay off the coast of Florida there is a giant Octopus with legs
the length of your body. It cradles the rocks, sheltering
beneath the water.

It has a memory that turns the way you
turn your head whenever you arrive at big bodies of water
and choose not to swim.

THE RULES OF ST. BENEDICT

Lauds, 4 bells

The concrete chapel is always cold because at the last minute, the monks changed their minds. The Architect wanted yellow. It would be his final touch: a trellis of stained-glass honeycomb facing east, looking down at the new highway opening up the prairie. He wanted red glass to match the native roses. His blue would be lakewater in August. But he needed the yellow to warm the chapel. In sketches he kept to himself, drawn on trains moving back and forth from St. Paul to St. Cloud, he traced the direction the sunlight would take. He watched it crawl up the hand of an old monk in prayer, lauding the day, the 4 a.m. waking. The chapel would breathe on its own.

Sext, 1956

The old dairy barn still smelled like hay. The monks and students shuffled between slabs of honeycomb glass laid out in the empty stalls, tapping paintbrushes against the transparent windows, filling them with the colors of the liturgical year: purple, blue, green, white, red, and a hint of gold. It was better this way, the monk who studied Art History explained. Even with the buzzing lights turned on overhead, the glass swallowed the light. Nobody noticed but one student worried he was doing it all wrong. Brother Mark walked past. The student looked down at his purple glass, swelling, he thought, like the dead cow in his father's barn last Christmas. The Abbey bells rang once for lunch and someone opened the doors to step outside. Light touched the stained glass for the first time and hurried past.

Vespers, 2009

At midnight the monks are sleeping, and we are awake, walking past the honeycomb wall of dark glass. The distance between our footsteps and the highway is measured by the wind. There are other students roaming the sidewalk outside their dorms. Nobody smells hay where the cows used to sleep. We are going down to the lake to swim, past the chapel towards the water. Someone's phone rings. When she pulls it from her pocket it lights up our path and we notice the time on the screen. Later than we'd realized. Later we will walk away shivering from the lake, away from the chapel, further down the highway, the way the Architect walked away from his unfinished masterpiece and left the monks to their hours, blinking awake, walking into the cold chapel each morning, praying in the colorless dawn.

WALKING WITH BASHŌ AT DUSK

The shape of cherry blossoms lost
in the dark.

We do not speak about
last season.

The snowy mountains
are only metaphors for the places
we cannot go.

Bashō has cold skin
that rings in the moonlight.

I tell him I have a home
where moss no longer grows.

OUT OF AUGUST

Because the back of your mind is like an alpine meadow
you drive into the city for whiskey, *knife fight with the devil*

is the only answer before noon, before you ask the cowboy
hat at the center of the bar if he knows any pilots willing

to take you over the mountains to make photographs, to make
yellow, to make peaks into gaping holes. *Joy for limbs grown wild*

was the advice they never gave, before you climbed to where
the photographs landed, sliding down hills of bearberries

fogged by dream work and decision-making. This is not
settling, I have been anxious too, in disbelief,

the empty branches in their leaves. It recedes as you wait
for mountains to rearrange themselves in your sleep.

How do you go on catching it?
The tinder grass pulling back the sky.

What we mistake for truth, the moon moving closer.
O shattered dishes back in their cupboards.

O pine planks still with bark on the last day of summer,
where the light we keep beneath the moss keeps on

growing, where from here all I see are women
jumping into the sky.

LOLO PASS

This morning, I sent you West.

And I want you to know what's coming next.

How I crossed into Idaho that first morning,

after it rained in the valley, climbing

through a highway of yellow larch folded

into wet falling snow, the silence was white

under every tree. The silence exiled the previous

season. There were no other places after that.

I'm sending you that way because you stopped here.

And everyone stops here before they keep going.

THE MONTANA PAINTINGS

View from Deep Creek (1974)

There is enough view for a flood here. Look, how it would sit cupped between the trees and high July glaciers, those alpine veins with a century left to drain. That is all you can see through haze. That is all you can believe exists. In this decade, I do not exist. What exists. A car on the highway. Two kids in the backseat. The plastic grocery bags talking. They are going to arrive home to foxgloves. They are going to step into the heat.

Sheep at Deep Creek (1972)

Old fat sheep grazing beside the highway. Morning of smoke filter and nostalgia. This is the season when heat folds the mountains into a blurry fortress. It hides inside the pines. Everything you touch becomes a thirst. Everything you remember is a shadow backing into the cool valley.

The Old Lambert Ranch (1974)

Someone believed this view was the answer to why we are never satisfied. The hand-cut fences and empty hay fields. There is a barn filled with silence. The absence displaced by light. Was it biblical? The first plow displacing the meadow. The pine in the woodstove. The graveyard without headstones. All this lingering, this holding on.

LECTURE

Library of crested windows and damp leaves. There is an undergraduate snoring next to shelves of *Natural Sciences and Mathematics*. Holding pattern of mountain fog and half-reaped sorrow. Her gray tights are twisting in skinny black boots. Is she late for Biology? Hand cupped over hazel hair twined between leather and cushions. Yellow climbing in through the window, trying to emphasize, trying to taste the same marginalia in drowsy bindings, words overlapping words, trying to outlast the forecast.

The marginalia are sleeping. The mountains are sleeping. A husband goes on cutting branches from the mealy apple tree and says without warning *it's not good, look at all those snags*. Neighbor dogs barking through the fence make the leaves fall faster. Depression is between a thumb and a pointer finger wedged where a previous life stood up and watched the moon step backwards into the ocean. It is the song you can't stop singing even when the bloom is a dried seed passed over by the wind.

MT. FLØYEN

The funicular deposits us above the city
the plugged chimneys turn to matches
    and the matches into alphabets carried around
by men and women making sidewalks
    into ribbons played by their legs scratching
down notes for a record we hear only
    birds at this height, beating through jet streams
with twigs and feathers hoping to land
    among tourists practicing their vowels, O the
view is always a layer of trees capped
    by waves drifting between centuries, O the
city is always trying to burn while
    we clap for the art of men who set tracks
into the heart of this mountain.

A QUIETER VERSION OF THE APOCALYPSE

1. Don't confuse interest with desire. I spent the morning harvesting carrots. Behind my garden the summer mountains separate us from the rest of the world. The poplar leaves wrestle with the wind. Everyone suspects rain.

2. In 1903 the city of San Diego hired a modern-day rainmaker named Charlie Hatfield to end their drought. His experiments were so successful a deluge flooded the new city, killing twenty people. I envy a century who believes in magic.

3. 2015 was the hottest year on record.

4. 2014. We move to Missoula, Montana. Afternoon rains absorb the dust. Tinder gray leaves brush the sidewalk. Nobody told us the mountains would change color.

5. I believe in reincarnation when it's convenient. Drew says past lives travel in pairs. We resurface decades apart holding the same memory. You plant the sapling and I swing from the branches. In another life we might have been lovers.

6. In another life the sky is a god.

7. In another life our artifacts are (a) buried, (b) decomposed, (c) anonymous museum exhibits.

8. When I am 22 I think, I cannot bring children into this world. When I am 28, I catch myself making space for more bodies. I put them at the table, in the yard, between us. Sometimes they fit and the space is already warm. Sometimes I make lists of things to do before they arrive.

9. An intern at CNN uncovers a doomsday video created
   in 1980 by Ted Turner. It was the Cold War. Two dozen
   uniformed men and women play "Nearer, My God, to Thee"
   on the grainy White House lawn. It was meant to be played
   when the world ended. Imagine the world tipping open:
   a million televisions with the same image. A million faces
   tipped towards the sky.

10. If you were stranded on a desert island would you rather
    have a lifetime supply of water or the belief that you would
    never die?

11. Today the world doesn't end. It has blue and green. A dog
    barks at children walking to school. Everything is too easy
    to hide inside. When I drink coffee the possibility of tides
    rising is my own life swept away.

12. My first apocalypse was Y2K. I wanted my parents to
    stockpile food. Instead they left me at home with the radio
    and promised to be home after midnight. I wanted the
    world to end to prove them wrong.

13. I decide that I'll hide in places with plenty of water. If there
    are clouds and lakes I feel safer, as if part of the world isn't
    slipping away. When a heat wave moves across Montana it
    feels like the entire city is lifting towards the sky. If we don't
    catch on fire we'll blow away. Suddenly the parable about
    dust feels real.

14. There is a legacy in my family of success. Every decade our
    homes grow bigger and food goes through us. We inherit
    the work of centuries. I understand why we don't want to
    change.

HEBRIDES CROFTERS, 1841

Your islands hung overcast. The forests pulled back. Craggy earth bare from the wood removed to feed wars beyond the strip of each horizon. It lowered, fused together each night the line between water and sky. You turned your back on land beached without borders. Here the sea rushed the rocks. Your children gathered seaweed strips. You hung them from rafters. Whitefish bathed in brine. Lamb's wool caught in thistles. Stone walls sloping towards water. You returned each fallen rock to the wall, until the earth rose up around it, inheriting the outline of your work. Until the men beyond swept over and pushed you out to sea.

BIRDS OF PRAISE

First, there's the story where you get a single wish.

You sit on the grass next to the dirt road choosing.

You choose a god with red hair.

The one who visits during your second cup of coffee.

She traded you visions for verbs and never followed through.

Say more about what you lost before you were warned about this.

Say more poetry in the age of capitalism without apologizing.

How everything you fold into this version of yourself

is anxious to keep promises made to someone else.

Are you convinced the path forward is not without prayer?

Folding is another way of helping bread rise.

The reason for your request is the path of the living.

ERIK AND THE WHALE SKULL

This much is true. The jaw too, on shore.
Flakes of krill salt baking into bone.

He could crawl inside the skull on the sand,
follow curves where the brain used to be.

I still like to follow him back into the sea. A later September storm.
Grandmothers sinking into prehistoric dreams.

We don't remember who found it.
Waves still purple the morning after.
We watched him peer inside. There were things we couldn't say.

How it rolled through the streets at night.
The chipped bone dust on our cheeks in the morning.

Whoever trusted the sea?
Something died and sank deep.

ACKNOWLEDGMENTS

Thank you to Rachel Mennies and Texas Tech University Press for giving this book a home, and to the publications where these poems first appeared:

New England Review: "The Present Season," "Just Try to Put It Back," "Haruspex"

Bright Bones: Contemporary Montana Writing: "Prima Materia"

The Carolina Quarterly: "St. John's University," "Crofters"

Belleville Park Pages: "When Flight 235 Crashes into the Keelung River"

Poetry Northwest: "Interview with a Mining Engineer Just Now Realizing the Property Under Discussion Appears to Be a Glacier," "Interview with a Planet Nobody Realized Was Hiding Behind the Sun"

With a special thanks to Jennifer Chang at the *New England Review* for her encouragement.

Deepest thanks to my early mentors and readers: Mara Faulkner, Kathryn Kysar, Mark Conway, Betsy Bonner, Hadara Bar-Nadav, Chris Dombrowski, Holly Wren Spaulding, Natalie Peeterse, Amy Ratto-Parks, Debra Magpie Earling, Prageeta Sharma, Joanna Klink, Mary Szybist, Stefania Heim, and Chip Blake.

To my fellow Merriam Frontier Award judges, Lois Welch and Ginny Merriam, who published my chapbook, *Peregrine* (2015), and then invited me to join them for tea at the kitchen table.

Thank you to the Kunstnarhuset Messen artist in residency in Ålvik, Norway; the Scottish island of Berneray; the Spring Creek Project and Shotpouch cabin in Eugene, Oregon; the Arrowhead Regional Arts Council; the Savenac forest service cabin just off of

I-90 on the Montana border; the monks at the Saint John's Abbey Guesthouse in Collegeville, Minnesota; the University of Montana MFA program; and the Ridge Scholarship at the Institute of Health and Humanities, all of which provided essential spaces and funding for me to think and write over many years.

To the women who provided childcare for my young boys, you made these poems possible: Heather Hefter, Rebecca Brown, Emily Richey, and Mabel Goodmen.

To my high school history teacher, Frieda Hall, whose curiosity and encouragement taught me to love the complexity of history.

To friends who shared the experiences and ideas behind many of these poems: Andrea Doerr, Anna Zumbahlen, Nick Triolo, Rachel Mindell, Nik Chang Hoon, Ashleigh Leitch, Madeline Neenan, Kelsey Daly, Chanti Calabria, Linds Sanders, Bailey Zook, Emy Scherrer, Emily Richey, Carolyn Drazich, Jen Dietrich, Brian Christianson, Brandon Zook, and so many others. This book was shaped by your enthusiasm and curiosity spanning decades of friendship.

And all my time and love to my family, most tenderly, to John, and our children, Leo & Guthrie.

NOTES

"The Present Season" emerged from a writing prompt given by Ellen Sheffield during a Minnesota Book Arts class.

"Interview with a Man Who Knows the Mona Lisa is Following Him" includes the line "dirty, badly dressed and disagreeable," which comes from multiple sources quoting Jeanne Calment, who died in 1997 at the age of 122.

In "Report Book for Mining Engineers," the claim, "Homer had no word for metal," comes from *Man and Metals* (1932). Most italicized lines come from the *Report Book for Mining Engineers* (1895).

Italicized lines in "Interview with a Mining Engineer Just Now Realizing the Property Under Discussion Appears to Be a Glacier" come from the *Report Book for Mining Engineers* (1895).

SOURCES

Bennett, Jane. *Vibrant Matter: A Political Ecology of Things*, 2009.

Boland, Eavan. *Object Lessons: The Life of the Woman and the Poet in Our Time*, 1995.

Charleton, A. G. *Report Book for Mining Engineers*, 1895.

Christianson, John. *On Tycho's Island: Tycho Brahe, Science, and Culture in the Sixteenth Century*, 2002.

Crowe, Michael J. *Theories of the World: From Antiquity to the Copernican Revolution*, 1990.

Eliade, Mircea. *The Forge and the Crucible.* Translated by Stephen Corrin, 1962.

Greenberg, Arthur. *From Alchemy to Chemistry in Picture and Story*, 2006.

Jeans, Sir James. *The Stars in Their Courses*, 1931.

Kapil, Bhanu. *Ban en Banlieue*, 2015.

Rickard, T. A. *Man & Metals: A History of Mining in Relation to the Development of Civilization*, 1933.

Purdy, Jedediah. *After Nature: A Politics for the Anthropocene*, 2015.

Saulitis, Eva. *Many Ways to Say It*, 2012.

West, John D. *Maidenhood and Motherhood, or Ten Phases of Woman's Life: How to Protect the Health, Contribute to the Physical and Mental Development, and Increase the Happiness of Womankind*, 1887.

ABOUT THE AUTHOR

Jolene Brink was born and raised in northern Minnesota. Her poetry and prose have appeared in *Orion*, *New England Review*, *Poetry Northwest*, *The Carolina Quarterly*, *Southern Humanities Review*, and elsewhere. She received her MFA in Creative Writing from the University of Montana, where her first poetry chapbook, *Peregrine*, won the Merriam-Frontier Award. She currently works for the University of Minnesota.

AUTHOR PHOTO BY JEFF KENNEL

www.ingramcontent.com/pod-product-compliance
Lightning Source LLC
Chambersburg PA
CBHW022012080426
42733CB00007B/569